Mommy, What Is This?

tree

flower

grass

mushroom

leaf

bug

bird

rock

Mommy,
what is this?

This is a tree.

Mommy, what is this?

This is a flower.

Mommy,
what is this?

This is a bug.

Mommy, what is that?

That is a mushroom.

Mommy,
what is that?

That is a leaf.

Mommy, what is that?

That is a bird.

Let's learn more about Russia.

Beef stroganoff